Lucretius

The First and Second Books of Lucretius

Translated

Lucretius

The First and Second Books of Lucretius
Translated

ISBN/EAN: 9783337186074

Printed in Europe, USA, Canada, Australia, Japan

Cover: Foto ©Thomas Meinert / pixelio.de

More available books at **www.hansebooks.com**

THE

FIRST AND SECOND BOOKS

OF

LUCRETIUS

Translated

PRIVATELY PRINTED

1879

LONDON:

G. NORMAN AND SON, PRINTERS, MAIDEN LANE,

COVENT GARDEN.

PREFACE

THE following is a reprint of an attempt made long ago by the translators—" Audaces juventâ,"—to put into English verse a portion of the most original and remarkable of Latin poems. They have thought it possible that the reprint, which is not meant for the Public or the Critics, may interest a few of their friends.

Sir John Trelawny is responsible for the first Book; Sir Robert Collier for the second.

ON THE NATURE OF THINGS.

THE FIRST BOOK.

PARENT of the Æneadæ—delight
Of Gods and men—benignant Venus ! thou
Who 'neath the gliding spheres of Heaven adorns't
The ship-supporting main and fruitful lands ;
Since through thee is each living thing conceived,
And, risen into being, sees the light :
Thee, Goddess, flee the winds—the clouds flee thee
And thy approach ; to thee the dædal earth
Sends forth her fragrant flowers ; with tranquil smile
The sea looks up at thee, and Heaven's expanse
By storms unruffled shines with light diffused.
For when the year assumes its vernal garb,
And freed Favonius, increase-giving, rules,
Thee, Goddess, first, and thy new presence felt,
Smit with thy power, aërial birds confess :
Then thro' glad pastures maddened cattle bound,

Spurning the torrent's course ; won by thy charms
With amorous speed, where'er thy course inclines,
All animated nature follows thee :
In fine, thro' rapid streams, o'er mountain tops,
'Mid leafy haunts of birds and blooming fields,
Kindling sweet love within the breasts of all,
Thou biddest every glowing tribe transmit
From age to age its own vitality.

    Since thou alone the Universe control'st,
Nor aught of lovely or desirable,
Save at thy nod, partakes of light and life—
My Muse invokes thee her associate,
While she expounds Eternal Nature's Laws
To Memmius, my friend, whom thou wouldst see
Excel in learned lore all other men.
Therefore the more with sempiternal charms
Invest my words ; grant that the din of war
May cease meanwhile, subdued by land and sea.
For thou alone canst mortal men delight
With tranquil peace, since over battled hosts
Armed Mars presides, who oft falls on thy breast,
By Love's eternal tribulation torn :
When looking up, his taper neck reclined,

Gazing on thee he feeds his eager looks,

Whilst on thy lips his glowing spirit dwells ;

Throw, Goddess, round his form thy sacred arms,

And from thy lips, Renown'd One, pour sweet plaints,

Imploring gentle peace may rest on Rome.

For, 'midst distracting cares of warlike strife,

My Muse cannot her placid course pursue ;

Nor should the offspring of a noble line,

E'en for Philosophy, forsake the State.

And now, my friend, lend me attentive ears ;

From cares estranged, explore true Reason's paths,

Nor spurned reject, before yet understood,

These gifts for thee with studious care prepared.

For 'tis my purpose to unfold, at large,

The laws of Heaven, the nature of the Gods,

The elements primordial of things

Whence Nature forms, augments, and nourishes

Her products, which, in course prescribed, resume

Their simple state called Matter ; primal germs,

Because from these all forms material spring.

But to the nature of the Gods belongs

Immortal Life, enjoyed in peace profound,

From every human care remote ; with them

Nor pain nor danger dwells; each passion sleeps
Serene, with native gifts content; applause
No merits win, no vice provokes to wrath.

When human life lay trampled under foot,
Borne down on earth by fell Religion's might,
Which from Heaven's highest realms its head
    displayed,
Daunting with horrid aspect mortal man;
Against it first a Greek was bold to raise
The eyes of men, and first to curb its sway;
Whom not the fame nor lightning of the Gods,
Nor Heaven's murmured threats could e'er restrain;
But these the more in him the valorous will
Aroused to be the first to burst the bars,
And open wide Eternal Nature's gates.
Thus has mind's vivid force prevailed, and far
Advanced beyond the flaming bounds of space,
And with bold thought explored the whole Immense,
Whence he, a victor, brings us back report
What may, what may not, into being spring;
How each thing has its force and limits fixed.
Thus bruised, in turn, lies Faith beneath our feet,
And victory exalts us to the skies.

But here I dread lest haply thou should'st deem
Thou art misled by impious reasonings
Into the paths of crime—the opposite
To truth ! for oftener has Faith begot
Shameless and impious deeds ; what time the Chiefs
For fame elect, who ruled the Doric host
At Aulis met, the Trivian virgin's shrine
Stained foully with Iphianassa's blood.
When now the veil which decked the maiden's
    locks
From either cheek in equal portions flowed,
And she her grieving sire at the altar's side
Beheld, from whom the priests concealed the knife,
And at the sight each sad spectator wept ;
Speechless with fear she bent her suppliant knee,
Nor did it then avail her that the King
From her had first the name of Father heard :
For, borne by men, and trembling, was she dragged
Towards the shrine—not that, due rites performed,
She might return in Hymeneal state—
But, 'midst her bloom, unstained, might sorrowing fall
By impious slaughter at a parent's hand
To earn a fleet a prosperous destiny—
Sample of evil deeds by creeds enjoined.

Yet, may be, sometime terror-struck by tales
Of bards, thou would'st desire me to desist ?
But then my fancy might as well invent
Fictions, which might disturb your judgment calm,
And veil in gloom your future destiny.
With reason too.   Yet could men once foresee
In Death their certain term of woe, no more
Thus vainly would they brave the threats of Faith,
Constrained to dread in Death eternal pain.
For men still lie in ignorance profound
On the essential nature of the Soul ;
Or with the frame connate, or first at birth
Infused ; and whether it become extinct
At Death, or whether Orcus' caverns vast
Receive it ; or, by agency Divine,   ,
It seek in turn the various forms of beasts,
As sung our poet Ennius, who first
From Helicon a crown unfading won,
Glorious alike to him and to his race.
And yet he too describes, in strains sublime,
The palaces of dismal Acheron,
Where souls nor bodies sojourn such as ours,
But certain pallid shadows ever glide ;
Whence, he relates, the ghost of Homer rose—

Immortal Bard !—and, as the salt tears flowed,
To him at full expounded Nature's laws.

Wherefore, 'tis meet our argument advert
Not only to the Gods, and to the laws
By which the Sun and Moon their courses hold,
And earthly forms into existence spring,
But also to the nature of the Soul,
And awe-inspiring phantasies which crowd
Our thoughts, in fevers wakeful, or in dreams,
So that we seem to see and hear the dead,
Whose bones the earth within her bosom holds.

Well knows my Latin Muse her arduous task—
Her subject new, her tongue as yet unskilled
In terms of art,—whilst she unfolds at large
Doctrines obscure, by Grecian sages taught.
Thy worth, with hoped-for joy of friendship sweet,
Makes labour light, whilst I, thro' nights serene,
Essay to choose fit words and worthy strains,
Such as may to thy mind impart clear light
By which thou mayest hidden causes search.

The native darkness of the Soul, perturbed

By craven fears, no lucid shafts of day
May penetrate, but Reason's power alone,
Of which this is a fundamental truth :
Nought, e'en by act Divine, from nothing springs.
In truth, a certain awe possesses men
As they behold the changes of events,
For which, lest such should causeless seem, they feel
Constrained to own an origin Divine.
But once concede that nought from nothing springs,
And straight we clearly trace each consequence,
Both whence the rise and bounds of things create,
And how events succeed without the Gods.

But if from nothing aught could spring, each form
Might also spring from each distinct in kind.
First, from the sea might men arise, from earth
Each sort of fish ; then from the sky might birds
Break forth ; sheep, cattle, every sort of beast
Would find their place, in waste or fruitful clime,
By chance alone ; the fruit of trees would change
Inconstant ; whilst on all all sorts might grow.
Forsooth, if things had not peculiar germs,
How then should kinds from kinds so certain spring
As they so spring, in fact, by certain laws,

But there appearing to the light of day,
Where first are found parental germs of each ?
Forms then spring not from forms distinct in kind,
Each has, in truth, but one productive source.

Why should the rose the Spring, the Summer corn
Prefer, the vine in Autumn flow alone :
But that fit germs then opportunely meet,
And everything create create appears
At its own season, when the fruitful earth
Can trust its tender buds to light of day?
If out of nothing things could sudden spring,
No more would they fixed seasons need for growth ;
As being without those germs primordial,
Whose confluence ungrateful climes might mar.

Nor, further, would the growth of things require
A period fixed, could they from nothing spring ;
For children would at once to manhood grow,
At once would shrubs ascend to tallest trees :
Against experience, since by degrees
Defined alone maturity is won ;
For the accrescence of its elements,
In each peculiar, conserves each kind.

Nor could the earth, unless by rain refreshed
At seasons due, its joyous harvests yield;
Of food deprived, each race of animals
Would fail to be renewed, and be extinct.
Hence, then, confess that all created things
Partake of certain common elements,—
As vary words, whose letters are the same,—
And nothing, but for these, could e'er exist.

Moreover, might not nature frequent bear
Gigantic men, such as should wade the deep,
And with their hands whole mountains rend in
    twain,
Surpassing, too, the usual term of life,
But that the substance each partakes is fixed,
By law determining what may arise?
From nothing, therefore, nothing can emerge,
Each form requiring generative germs,
By which alone it breathes the air of day.

And since we see the meadow far exceed
The waste, and ever yield the richer crop,
Needs must we own the earth contains the germs
Of products which, when plough-share first upturns

The fruitful soil, we summon forth to life ;
And, but for these, each form spontaneous,
Without our toil, superior far might grow.

Think not, whilst forms decay, their germs become
Extinct; these re-assume their primal state.

Indeed, if such could mortal be throughout,
Each form might sudden vanish from our sight,
And no disruptive force would be required
To cause decay, and sever parts conjoint.
But, since each form contains eternal parts,
It cannot perish, under Nature's law,
Till subtle forces penetrate the mass,
And, severing the parts, dissolve the frame.

Besides, could Time annihilate the germs
Of forms which their allotted term fulfil,
How thence could Venus from extinction save
The race of animals ; or, how the Earth
By nourishment support her tender charge ?
How could each native spring supply the Sea,
Each river's serpent course ? or ether feed
The stars of Heaven?   The past would have consumed

All matter, were it to extinction prone.
But, if thro' all that period vast elapsed,
The sum of things has ever been the same,
It must be from mortality exempt.
Therefore, to nothing, nothing can return.

Again, unless Eternal matter held
The parts of things more close conjoined in some
Than others, then one force might all destroy.
Extinction might succeed the lightest touch;
For, were no parts from dissolution free,
Some force might then the closest texture mar.
But now, because textures dissimilar
Bind concrete forms whose substance is eterne,
Their bulk remains inviolate, till force
O'erpower their several coherency.
Nought then to nothing can return; when things
Decay, they seek their primal elements.

But rain is lost, soon as the Father Air
Has poured it on the lap of Mother Earth?
But thence bright crops arise, and branches bloom
On trees; these gather strength, and teem with fruit.
Hence, too, Man's race, and animals are fed;

Hence we behold our towns with children swarm,
Whilst with young birds each leafy grove resounds;
The sated herd their wearied frames repose
'Midst joyous fields, and from distended teats
The candent liquid streams; their young, refreshed,
With wanton gambols mar the tender blade.
Thus Nature merely moulds anew what seems
To be extinct; each new-made form in turn
Dissolves, and yet no part is ever lost.

And, that thou may'st not rash withhold assent
When I assert that nothing springs from nought,
And that to nothing, nothing can return,
Because we cannot see primordial germs—
Hear now what forms thou must of force admit
Exist in things, and yet cannot be seen.

For first, the Winds, aroused, disperse the clouds,
Roll up the deep, and shatter navies vast;
Sometimes they scour the plain with torrent course,
Strewing it far and wide with levelled trees,
Whilst wooded hills moan 'neath the splintering blast—
With such might rage the Winds, by land and sea.
Doubtless, because unseen material forms

Sweep over sea and earth, and bear along,
In whirlwind course, the harassed clouds of sky;
So speed the gales, their path with ruin strewn;
As when a gentle brook is sudden swoln
By tributary streams, which recent floods
Pour from the mountain on the plain below,
Bearing the spoils of forests in their course;
Nor can strong bridges break th' united force
Of rushing waters: with such boisterous might
The turbid current shakes each trembling mass,
Which falls with loudest crash; whilst stones, in
    vain
Resisting, roll along beneath the waves.
Thus, therefore, like a mighty stream, the Winds
Their course pursue, and with impetuous gusts
O'erwhelm whatever thwarts their headlong flight,
Nor speed abate, but oft, with tortuous course,
Snatch up, and whirling, bear away their prey.
Wind, then, consists of parts material;
For as, in its effects, it rivals streams,
It must, like them, partake of solid bulk.

Then, further, various odours strike the sense,
And yet these in their course escape our sight.

Heat, cold, and sound lurk hidden to the eye ;
And yet all these must be material,
Since they, by contact, agitate the nerves—
For body only can be touched, or touch.
Clothes, too, hung high above wave-breaking shores,
Grow damp ; in sunny warmth outstretched, they dry ;
Tho' all unseen, both how they first imbibe,
And then how Heat exhausts, the dewy spray ;
Doubtless, because the fluid is reduced
To parts impalpable to human eye.

Again, a ring, upon the finger worn,
Grows less as Sol renews the circling years ;
To dropping water stone gives way ; the plough
Wastes, unobserved, its crooked tooth i' the soil ;
We see our stone-laid pavements trodden smooth ;
Our brazen statues, standing near our gates,
Show one hand smoothed, by greetings frequent paid,
Or pious reverence of passers-by.
So far may loss of substance be discerned,
Though Nature jealously precludes our view
Of each receding particle of bulk.

Besides, the keenest eye must fail to scan

Each single atom which, by Nature's art
Constrained, adapts itself to growing forms;
Or which, in turn, becomes disjoined by age,
Or wan disease; or where huge cliffs impend
The main, by rock-devouring brine dissolved.
Therefore, we must admit that Nature moulds
Or mars her works by agency unseen.

And yet think not that matter sole pervades
The whole Immense, since there is Space besides,—
A truth it much imported thou should'st know,
And which will banish far vain thoughts and doubts,
About some undefined Sum of Things,
Raising distrust of these my reasonings.
Now Space, defined, is Place of Matter void.

Without this Motion were impossible,
For body, which implies resisting force,
Would progress intercept on every side,
Since progress without space could not begin.
Whereas, by sea, by land, 'midst Heaven's high vault,
We daily see all kinds of forms partake
Of motions various, which, but for space,
Not only would of motion be deprived,

But never could, in fact, have been at all,
Since matter would have lain compressed, inert.

Nor are the parts of things which densest seem
So dense that they allow no space between.
In caves, pure water may be seen to flow
From rocks whose droppings seem like tears to fall;
Food thro' the body is distributed;
Trees grow, and in due season yield their fruit,
Because their roots supply fit nutriment,
Which is diffused throughout each trunk and branch;
Voices thro' walls are heard, through houses barred
They fly; cold's rigour penetrates the bones.
Impossible, but that the particles
Of each sufficient space for transit find.

And why, I pray, should things predominate
In weight o'er others, differing not in size?
For, if like bulk of wool and lead contain
Like body, then their weight must be the same,
Because alike all matter downward tends,
While contrary space without weight subsists.
Therefore, of equal bulks, the lighter found

2

Plainly contains the more of vacant space ;
The heavier has greater wealth of germs,
Containing less of vacuum within.
Therefore sagacious reason must admit
That with all body there is blended space.

And here beware an argument advanced,
On evidence unsound, though plausible,
By those who say the sea receding yields
The scaly tribe a passage thro' the deep,
Because each fish behind it leaves a space
Wherein the brine displaced reverts to rest,
And that thus other forms may no less move,
Though matter solely fill the Universe.
In vain : for how should fish advance, unless
The waters yielded space ? or water move,
The fish the while restrained in state of rest ?
Thus Motion must to body be denied ;
Or else we must admit a vacuum,
By which alone it ever could begin.

Moreover, if two polished surfaces
Are sudden drawn apart, the air without
At once attempts to fill the space between.

And yet, tho' favoured by conspiring winds
Around, it cannot simultaneously
Fill all the space: for it must occupy
Each part before it can possess the whole.

But if one say it might possess the whole
At once, because the air becomes condensed,
Then that would void become, which was not void,
And that be filled, which was a void before.
Air cannot, as assumed, be thus condensed;
And if condensed, it could not without space
Have all its parts thus drawn into itself:
Thus, spite of hours in cavil vain misspent,
Needs must thou grant a vacuum exists.

In short, I might, by many reasons more
Add force to what has been already urged;
But I forbear.   Your prompt sagacity
Requires no further clue to know the rest:
As mountain-ranging hounds full oft disturb
The copse-protected lair of some fierce beast,
Whose errant track they once have scented out,
So may you in this argument from step
To step advance, till you have quite explored
Truth's dark retreat, and brought her forth to day.

But should'st thou fail at first to apprehend
Each novel view, this pledge at least accept,
My Memmius; fed from our Fountain deep,
My fertile tongue shall from my soul pour forth,
In accents sweet, such copious draughts of lore
That I may fear lest thro' each limb old Age
Should halting creep and ope the gates of life,
Ere these my strains have to your ears conveyed
What any single topic might suggest.
The more, then, to our subject let us haste.

All Nature, in her first and simplest state,
Comprised two elements; Material forms,
And Space, in which these move and being have;
The former to sensation palpable,
On which, should we not place implicit faith,
No standard of opinion remains
To found belief, or regulate assent;
The latter, Place, or, as we call it, Space,
Were it nowhere, nowhere could bodies be,
Nowhere could they in various ways be moved,—
A truth by recent arguments enforced.

Moreover, Nature no third element

Contains from body as from space distinct.
For were there such, when it began to be,
It must have had or more or less of size; `
Which, if it could endure the lightest touch,
Tho' small its bulk, to Body would belong ;
But could it not be touched, nor yet resist
Whatever might thro' it attempt to pass,
It then would plainly be what we call Space.

Whatever, too, exists, must either act,
Or else be passive to extraneous acts,
Or suffer acts performed within its bounds.
Now Body only bears, or acts itself ;
Space only suffers acts within its bounds.
Therefore, no other native quality
Remains besides, save only Body and Space ;
Whether of things of which our senses judge,
Or which the mind, by taking thought, conceives.

Whatever else is called an entity
Must be of these an adjunct or event ;
The former marking some condition fixed,
Essential to its subject's permanence.
Thus, Stones are heavy, Water moist, Fire burns,

Body is tangible, while Space is not.
But Liberty, and Slavery, and Wealth,
War, Poverty, and Peace—states transient—
By which, present or absent, Nature still
Remains unchanged,—all such are called Events.

Time, of itself, is nothing ; but the Mind
Observes, in things themselves, what has transpired,
What now exists, what will hereafter be ;
And no one can take cognizance of Time
But from the mutability of things.

And when we hear of Helen's ravishment,
And how the Trojans were subdued in war,
Such facts must not be said to be themselves,
Since all the men by whom these acts were done
Relentless Past has long since borne away.
Whatever has been done at any time
Is an Event of persons or of things

In fine, had Matter never been at all,
Nor Place, nor Space, in which events occur,
The glowing flame, in Phrygian Paris' breast
By the fair form of Tyndaris lit up,

Could never have aroused such conflicts dire;
Nor could the wooden monster have brought forth
Those hidden Greeks who buried Troy in flames.
And hence observe that great exploits achieved
Cannot, like Matter, unsupported stand,
Or be, as Space is often said to be;
But these are rather what are called Events
Of Body and of Place, where they are done.

Body sometimes preserves its simple state,
Sometimes its parts cohere, and blend in forms.
But no one atom is divisible;
Their solid forms no force can overcome.
And if known facts should seem to contradict
That bodies purely solid should exist—
For lightning penetrates the thickest walls;
So sounds of human tongue; iron grows white
In fire; and glowing stones in splinters fly;
Gold's rigid temper heat disintegrates;
Brass, too, runs molten 'midst the conqu'ring flame;
But silver cold as well as heat pervades,
As, when we lift the bowl, our hands discern
The water poured within, or hot or cold;
And thus, in Nature, nothing solid seems :—

Attend, I pray, since Truth requires thus much,
While briefly in these verses I expound
How those Eternal solid forms may be,
Which we have called primordial elements :
Because they form the Sum of Things create.

Now, first, since it appears the Universe
Contains two opposites, Body and Space,
For, without Space, Events could not occur,
Each must subsist alone, and be distinct :
For where pure Space exists, which we call void,
There Body is not : again, where matter is,
There Space, too, clearly, cannot co-exist.
Thus, therefore, primal forms are void of Space.

Since, too, some things in part consist of Space,
It must by solid Matter be inclosed :
Indeed, it were a vain attempt to prove
That any concrete form has Space within
Unless we grant the solid bounds the void.
Of these, the solid can but represent
Collected parts primordial, bounding Space.
And note, that parts thus solid must exist
Throughout all Time, while concrete forms decay.

Further, if Space nowhere existed pure,
The Universe would be one solid whole ;
Again, if no material forms fill up
The bounds assigned them, all must be a void.
Therefore, alternately, since the Immense
Is neither wholly full, nor wholly void,
Matter and Space distinct exist ; the first
Being only found in primal elements.

The forms of these yield not to blows without ;
No subtle force an entrance finds within ;
E'en Art assailing, they destruction shun—
Unfolded this, and proved in earlier verse.
For nothing, without Space between its parts,
Can suffer fracture, or be rent in twain :
Solids resist destructive elements,
Or treacherous cold, or moist, or subtle heat.
In truth, the less of Space a form contains,
So much less likely it will be dissolved.
Thus, therefore, solid forms, being destitute
Of Space within, needs must eternal be.

Besides, could Matter perish, then all things
Alike might have, ere this, returned to Nought,

From which things now existing must have sprung.
But since it has been proved that Nothing springs
From Nought, and that to Nothing Nought returns,
There must exist Eternal elements,
To which decaying forms may be reduced;
And whence, in turn, their loss may be supplied.
These are the simple solid elements,
By which alone, thro' ages infinite,
Nature could have sustained the Universe.

  Again, if the divisibility
Of matter had no term by Nature fixed,
Its part would be so much reduced by Time
That Nothing, by their confluence conceived,
Could in due season reach the pride of bloom;
For ever things more rapidly decay
Than they are formed.   And thus the boundless tract
Of all-disturbing, all-dissolving Time
Would never have allowed the fragile forms
It once had marred to be renewed at all.
But now, in truth, Decay has been restrained
By bounds defined.   We see each form renewed,
Within some certain time, and, once renewed,
At its own time attain maturity.

And here observe that, tho' primordial germs
Are purely solid, yet of these soft things,
Air, water, earth, or heat, may be create,
Since with these bodies space is intermixed.
But, were primordial germs by Nature soft,
No means could be assigned whence flinty rocks,
Or iron, might be made.   Nature would want
A sure foundation for her works begun.
Still, then, there must be simple solid forms,
Of which, condensed, the hardest substances,
And least to dissolution prone, consist.

Moreover, since each living creature born
Has its allotted time for growth and life,
And since the Laws of Nature have defined
What may, what may not, into being spring,
And since these never change, but operate
So constantly that all the several kinds
Of birds preserve their wonted plumage gay;
The substance out of which they spring must be
Immutable.   For, if primordial germs
Subdued by violence could suffer change,
It might thenceforth remain in doubt what might,
Or what might not, arise; in short, what powers

Assigned each natural agent might exert ;
Nor would each race repeat its type unchanged,
Like in their natures, motions, habits, food.

   Then, further, since there is a point extreme
Of each material form impalpable
To human eye, it must be without parts,
Being itself the very Least of Things,
Which never did, or shall, exist distinct
From that whose first and smallest part it is.
Now similar particles, each joined to each,
In dense assemblage fill up every germ ;
And, since they cannot be alone, they must
Cohere, with force that nothing overcomes,
Which argues solid every primal form ;
Since each consists of these the least of things
Condensed, but that not by affinity
Of parts, but as their first and simple state,
In which they were by Nature made exempt
From all decay, that germs might be entire.

   Besides, if there were not a minimum,
The smallest things might have parts infinite ;
For every part would always have its half,

Nor would such subdivision have an end.
Then how would differ objects large and small?
They would not differ : for tho' infinite
The Universe in parts, yet so each part
The smallest would be likewise infinite.
But since a reasoning soul will not admit
This attribute, we are constrained to own
That there may be forms wholly void of parts,
The Least by Nature ; which, if they exist,
Must likewise Solid and Eternal be.

Again, could Nature not resolve her works
Into their first and simple elements, .
Decaying forms could never be renewed,
Because each mass composed of many parts
Would want the reproductive quality
Dependent on the impact, motion, weight,
And form of each, while in its separate state.

Although, too, the divisibility
Of Matter had no certain term defined,
Yet that some forms still undissolved remain
From all Eternity, our senses prove :
But were all things alike of fragile mould,

Harassed and tossed about time without end,
E'en these would not survive the shocks received.

  And as to those who hold the Universe
Consists of one, its sole ingredient, Fire,
Far have they wandered from true Reason's paths.
First in the van stands Heraclitus, famed
Amongst some triflers fond of doubtful terms,
But ill-received by Greeks who sought the truth.
For fools admire and praise the most conceits
Dimly perceived and clothed in words obscure,
And, won by elegance of sound, mistake
For true whatever fascinates the ear.

  For whence this great variety of forms,
I ask, if all consist alone of Fire?
Nor would it profit them to say that Fire
Sometimes contracts, sometimes dilates its parts,
If each contain the essence of the whole.
For, though Fire might more fiercely glow, condensed,
And waste its energy when rarefied,
Yet could no greater change than this be deemed
To flow from causes such as these; still less
The great variety of forms we see.

If, too, these men would grant a vacuum
Exists, they might consistently assert
That Fire may be condensed or rarefied ;
But, dreading lest they should refute themselves,
They pause amidst conflicting doubts, and lose,
By their timidity, the way to Truth.
Nor can they understand that, but for Space,
The Universe would be a solid mass,
Which never could emit aught from itself,
As glowing fire sends forth both light and heat.

But then, perchance, it might be urged the parts
Of Fire might in their concourse cease to be,
Their bounds engrossed by new formed substances ;
Then Fire, in truth, to Nothing might return,
Whence also each new thing create would spring :
For that which loses some essential mark
Of what it was ceases at once to be.
Now Nothing altogether perishes,
For else might all alike return to Nought,
And out of Nought renewed abundance rise.

Since, too, there are primordial elements,—
Certain unchangeable, material forms,

By whose departure, access, new array,
The nature of each thing remains the same,—
These, be assured, cannot consist of Fire.
For what would it avail that they depart,
Or come, or frequently their order change,
If all, by Nature, still consist of Fire?
For out of Fire Fire only could be born.
In fine, there must be certain primal germs,
Whose concourse, order, motion, figure, place,
Engender Fire, which changes when they change,
Their mutual relations fixed; now these
Neither resemble Fire, nor aught beside,
Which from its mass can send forth other forms,
And by their contact agitate the sense.

To say, indeed, that all things are but Fire,
And that this element alone exists,
Which these same men contend, is but to rave;
For they employ the senses to confute
The senses—upon which all knowledge rests—
Even of that which has the name of Fire.
For in the case of Fire, the senses rule;
Distrusted yet in things as palpable.
A vain and foolish conduct of the mind!

What evidence have we of true or false—
What standard—not upon our senses based ?

Why should we take away all other things,
And say that one sole element exists,
More than deny this one, and leave the rest ?
For either would be equally insane.

Wherefore, those who have thought the Universe
Consists of one, its sole, ingredient, Fire ;
And those who hold all Nature is but Air ;
Or those who say Water might, of itself,
All products generate ; or, lastly, Earth
Might into other natures be transformed :
Widely all seem to deviate from Truth.

And no less those who blend two elements,
In one, as Fire with Air, with Water Earth ;
Or who maintain that of these four combined,
Air, Water, Earth, and Fire, all things are formed :—

Of whom the Agragantine was the chief,
Empedocles ; whose native isle extends
Its triple promontories 'mid the waves,

Round which the dark blue rolling deep sends up
From breakers vast the salt Ionian spray,
And from whose cliffs a narrow stormy strait
Divides the sister shores of Italy.
Hard by, is vast Charybdis : and not far
In murmurs Etna threatens gathered wrath,
And from her jaws flames vomited anew,
And lightnings shot again thro' Heaven's high vault ;
A region which, tho' rich in every gift
Admired by man,—for wealth, for citizens,—
Yet nothing had more noble, precious, grand,
More hallowed, or more marvellous, than him
Whose soul sublime bespeaks the mind in strains
So clear, melodious, divine, that thou
Would'st deem him sprung from more than mortal
    stock.

   Yet even he, as well as others named
Already, but to him inferior,
Although they have, as from a shrine, poured forth
Responsive Wisdom from their gifted breasts,
And words more sound, and far less impious,
Than Pythian priestess at Apollo's fane
From tripod and from sacred laurel spake,—

Falsely conceived the Elements of Things,
And, with their chief, in common ruin fell.

For, first, they hold that bodies may be moved
Without a vacuum, and that soft things,
As Air, the Sun, Fire, Earth, Corn, Animals,
Need not have Space within their substance
    mixed.

Then, they will have Matter divisible
Into parts infinite ; and disallow
That there can be a point least possible ;
When yet, of each thing seen, there is some point
Which seems to be the very least of things ;
From which one may conclude the points extreme
Of things unseen must be, in fact, the least.

They, too, think primal germs by nature soft ;
Such as we know that forms alone can be,
Which may be concrete, and dissolved by turns.
Then might the Universe sometimes become
Extinct, sometimes spring up again from nought ;
Both which, how far removed from Truth, thou
    know'st.

3 *

Their elements, moreover, are opposed,
And mutually destructive, each to each;
Or, if combined, soon would they fly apart,
Scattered as storms of thunder, wind, and rain.

Further, if of four Elements all Things
Are made—to which all are again resolved,—
Why should these four be rather Elements
Of Things create, than, converse, these of them?
For they, alternately, exchange their states;
Each takes the other's nature, colour, form.
But, haply, if thou deem'st that Earth and Air,
And Fire and Water, may together blend,
And yet preserve their diverse characters,
Nothing organic could be formed of them;
Nor creatures having souls, nor those without:
For each, in such a heap confused, would show
Its proper essence; nothing would appear
But mingled Fire and Water, Air and Earth.
In short, primordial parts of concrete forms
Must not submit their qualities to sense,
Lest these appearing should deprive the forms,
Wherein they chance, at times, to congregate,
Of their own private essences distinct.

Then they deduce three of their Elements
From yon bright orbs which blaze amid the sky ;
Supposing Air derivative from these ;
Water from Air ; and then, from Water, Earth,
From whence Fire gradually proceeds again ;
And, thus, that Elements inconstant share
Each other's native qualities, which ought
To be incapable of change in each ;
For else might everything return to nought.
For when an Element bounds oversteps
By Nature once assigned, that ceases then
To be which was before ; so that Earth, Air,
Water, and Fire could not be changed at all,
But that they change the germs which they contain,
These being, thro' all Time, immutable ;
For else, again might all return to nought.
The rather, then, conclude that germs like these
Haply combining in the form of Fire,
By their departure, access, order, changed,
May blend in other compounds, such as Air.

But then, thou say'st, experience proves that plants
And animals spring forth to light, and draw
Their sustenance from Earth ; and that, unless

A mild and genial clime indulge their growth—
Which on due heat and moisture must depend—
Each flower and shrub would droop and pine away.
Doubtless: and, were not dry and liquid food
Supplied our frames, the principle of life
Would soon desert our bones and arteries:
For we, like other animals, extract
Due nourishment from certain articles
Of food, and those alone ; forsooth, because
In many things, many primordial parts—
To many others suitable—inhere,
And thus things are supported, each from each.
But then it much imports what sort of germs
Combine, and in what order they are placed,
What kind of impact they receive or give ;
For Elements not only form the Sea,
The Earth, the Sun, the Sky, but every kind
Of fruits or animals ; in which they are,
In divers ways, by divers motions, mixed.

And thus, for instance, in these very lines
Are many common elements of words,
When, yet, thou needs must own that both the lines
And words are different in sound and sense ;

So much depends upon mere change of place.
But much more various are the composites
In which material germs may be combined.

Learn, now, what Anaxagoras has taught,
The Homæomerist: a name 'mongst Greeks
In use, but in our barren tongue unknown,
Which yet affords fit words to state, in brief,
The fundamental doctrines of his school :—
That every form consists of forms minute
Resembling it ; that, for example, bones
Are but compounded particles of bone,
The same in kind ; again, that blood consists
Of particles minute of blood-like form ;
That gold is formed of parts resembling gold ;
And that Earth, Water, Air, and Fire, in short,
All things, consist of homogeneous parts.

He, too, and others, whose opinions
We have already weighed, would not concede
That Space exists ; and Matter he believed
Divisible into parts infinite.

Further, their Elements, if they retain

The nature of the composites they form,
Must be no less to dissolution prone ;
For how should they escape the common fate
Of all created things ? could Fire, or Air,
Could Water, Blood, or Bone, sustain itself?
Impossible : when nothing is exempt
From the decrees of stern Mortality.
But we have proved nothing returns to nougi.',
And that from nothing nought can spring anew.

And, since the body is sustained by food,
The essence of our veins and blood must be
Distinct from that by which they are supplied ;
Nor can they say that various kinds of meat
Contain the homogeneous elements
Required to form our blood and arteries ;
For then it could not be maintained that food
Itself consists of homogeneous parts.

Moreover, if those forms which spring from earth
Be in their parts complete before they grow,
Then earth itself would merely be a mass
Of elements from earth dissimilar.

Again, if wood comprises ashes, flame,
And smoke, how then is wood itself defined?

Here subtly reasons Anaxagoras,
Who, wanting grounds assured, maintains all kinds
Of forms lurk unperceived within the bounds
Of each; which there seems individual,
Where certain parts in greatest number meet,
And lie most palpably exposed to view:
Refuted this by Nature's plainest law,
For then would corn, when ground within the mill,
Discover latent particles of blood;
Which in due time supply the human frame.
Each herb would show the nature of the juice
It bears within its cells; whence milk would flow
As sweet and fresh as from the fleecy ewe;
Then earth, reduced to dust, would show the parts,
Dispersed, and almost imperceptible,
Of every kind of grass and corn and leaves;
And thus, in wood might ashes, flame, and smoke,
Nay more, the subtle parts of fire, be seen,
Of which, since we have no experience,
We may at once deny that parts minute
Resembling every kind exist in each,

And still maintain that many elements,
Common to many things, conspiring form
The infinite variety we see.

But, sayest thou, when now the southern blast
Begins to sweep along the mountain side,
The tops of neighbouring trees full oft ignite ?
Doubtless ; but yet think not fire lurks in wood,
But certain germs, by violence aroused,
Conspire, by chance, and take the form of fire.
For, if in wood flames really might subsist,
How should they be for any time concealed ?
Long since each forest would have been consumed.

And here take note again, it much imports
What kind of germs combine ; what order they
Assume ; what impact they receive or give :
For germs combining form each organism,
As the same letters, differently arranged,
Form words which signify distinct ideas.

Lastly, if you conceive the composites
We see could never have been formed, unless
We first assume primordial elements

Resembling them : we might as well pretend
Laughter is but the prevalence of germs
Resembling it, and grief of others, which
With copious floods of tears bedew the checks.

Learn now, I pray, what still remains unsung.
My subject well I know obscure ; and yet,
Great hope of praise has with keen thyrsus stung
My heart, and sweet love of the Muses struck
Within : so armed, with eager mind, I track
The pathless haunts of the Pierides
Untrod by foot before.   For thus I love
To seek the limpid fount and quench my thirst ;
I love to gather flowers newly blown,
And from the Muses earn a coronal
Whence, yet, they never decked the brow of man.
For, first, I teach great truths unknown before,
And strive to free the faith-enthralled mind
From galling chains by superstition forged.
Then I array thoughts dark and difficult
In lucid verse, with labour not misspent :
As, when Physicians would beguile a child
To drink the bitter wormwood draught, they first
The cup with sweet and yellow honey tint,

That his unguarded age may be deceived
Lip-far at least, meanwhile the cup is drained
Of its contents, and thence no harm ensues,
But rather, by this practice, health returns.
So now, since my philosophy may seem
Gloomy to the unlettered, and the herd
E'en with aversion spurn it, I essay
To chasten its severity by verse,
Tinging its surface with Pierian sweets,
The better thus to win attentive ears
While I expound the Rest of Nature's laws.

And since we know that solid primal germs
Their courses hold eternally in Space,
It next may be inquired are they finite
Or infinite; and whether Place or Space,
Wherein Events succeed have bounds defined,
Or else towards the vast extend Immense?

That which comprises all the Sum of Things
Cannot itself have bounds, for, were there such,
They would appear beyond what they confine;
But that which is, the Sum of Things includes:
Therefore, the Universe is infinite;

For, though the Mind extend its scope afar
Beyond this narrow World, it can conceive
No bound that is not of the whole a part.

Besides, were there some point extreme of things,
Some distant region bounding Space, at which
A man might stand and hurl a winged dart,
Think'st thou it would, if cast with utmost force,
Fly where its point is turned ? or cease to fly,
Obstructed by some barrier without ?
Or this, or that, needs must thou one admit,
Though either bar escape, and prove the All
Lies open every way from bounds exempt—
Or whether anything impede the dart,
Preventing altogether farther flight,
Or whether it continue on its course.

If, too, the Universe had bounds defined,
By which it is inclosed on every side,
Borne down by weight, all matter would, ere now,
Have been deposited in state of rest ;
So that organic creatures must have ceased
To spring up under Heaven, the Sky itself
Would long have ceased to be, the Sun to glow ;

Nought would remain but one incongruous mass
Of solid forms, condensed, confused, inert.
But now we know that germs have no repose ;
No barrier arrests their downward flight ;
Besides, all kinds of objects daily spring,
In every region of the Earth, from germs
Ever and ceaseless confluent from Space.

And though Air terminates the mountain peak,
And land in turn defines the atmosphere,
Tho' Earth and Sea describe each other's bounds,
Yet nothing can define the Universe.
Its very nature is Immensity ;
As though some noble stream should wind its course
Perennial ; but never find its term,—
Which could not even be approached,—so wide,
So vast and boundless are the realms of Space,
On every side, above, around, below.

Then Nature proves her own Infinity :
For Space and Body everywhere supply
Each other's bounds : where either first begins
To fail, the other thence were Infinite.
If Space by Body ceased to be defined,

The Sea, the Earth, the Sky's refulgent dome,
The race of Man, the essence of the Gods,
Could not survive a moment's fleeting course :
Their primal Elements would diverse fly,
Disorganized, throughout the vast Inane ;
Or, rather, never could have form attained
In such uncertain confluence of germs.

For know primordial Elements assumed
Their present order without Providence,
Without the aid of all-disposing mind :
Urged here and there thro' ages infinite,
Every kind of impact, every change
Of motion, and new combination tried,
They fell, at last, into the ranks they hold,
And thus the Universe was organized :
Which, once complete, thro' periods vast, obeyed
Such laws as best insured its permanence ;
So that each river's constant course supplies
Insatiate Ocean ; whilst the kindling beams
Of Phœbus warm and fertilize the soil,
Which teems anew with animated life,
And Heaven glows with bright revolving fires ;
Which, were not germs in number infinite,

Would be impossible: decaying forms,
Thus unsupplied, could never be renewed.

For as, by Nature, every animal,
Of sustenance deprived, soon pines away,
So would the Universe itself dissolve,
Without accession of new particles.

Again, think not that concrete forms, composed
Of finite germs, could ever be preserved
By frequent impact of external parts,
So that some might be thus detained, till more
Might, by their presence, save all from decay;
For Force is ever followed by recoil,
And germs rebounding would afford both Time
And Space for the escape of particles,
Which were before compressed in various forms.
Germs, then, must be, in number, infinite;
The more, indeed, if they supply the force
By which, alone, each composite subsists.

But, more than all, avoid what some have taught,
That all things tend towards some central point:
That thus the Universe sustains itself

Without the force of circumjacent parts :
That bodies do not uniformly fall
In downward course precipitous in Space,
(As if it were not idle to suppose
Aught could sustain itself; and that each mass
Which lies the other side beneath the Earth,
Though tending upwards, still remains at rest,
As seem our shadows at the water's edge :)
And that all kinds of animals exist
Upon the lower surface of the World,
Which no more fall into the vault below
Than we ascend into the Sky above,
And which enjoy the light of day, when we
Discern the stars of night, and share with us,
In turn, the various seasons of the year.

All which has error vain for fools devised,
Because they first from Nature's teaching strayed :
For in unbounded Space there cannot be
A central point ; and could such point exist,
Why rather should all bodies thither tend
Than to some other region far removed ?
For every part of Space, however near
The centre, must afford to equal weights

4

Their unimpeded course.   Nor place exists
Within which bodies, sudden reft of weight,
Become for ever fixed and motionless :
For Space, whose very nature yields the power
To move, would never stay the course begun
Of any moving form.   The less believe
That things could in concerted order stand,
Subdued by passion for some central point.
Besides, it is not held that every kind
Of these alike to one fixed centre tend,
But only those which form the Sea and Earth,
And torrents flowing from the mountain ridge ;
Whilst those of which the Air and Fire consist
Forth from such centre fly; on which account,
The tremulous starry spheres incessant glow
Amid the Sky, fed by the gathering fires,
Which ever Heavenward bend their quivering light:
As Earth sustains the race of mortal men,
No less than trees which rear their lofty heads
Luxuriant with verdant foliage.
The same men falsely hold some barrier
Confines the Universe, lest all its parts
Should chance obtain an outlet, and escape
Into the infinite supernal void ;

And all the World within one moment cease
To be, and nought remain but simple Space.

Thus much, my friend, by generous toil attained,
No darkness shall arrest thy further course ;
(So much each step assured explains the next,)
E'en where the deepest truths of Nature lead.

THE SECOND BOOK.

'Tis sweet, when tempests heave the mighty main,
To view from shore the struggling seaman's toil ;
Not that man's suffering pleases, but the sense
Of our own freedom from the ills we see :
'Tis pleasant too to view from hill secure,
The clash of mighty hosts upon the plain :
But sweeter far, from the well guarded height
Of Wisdom's Temple, rear'd by sages' lore,
To look serene upon the throng below ;
To mark their restless wanderings all abroad
In quest near-ending of the way of life ;
Their rivalries in rank, in learned fame ;
Their daily, nightly struggles, unrelaxed,
For golden store and eminence of power.
Poor blinded mortals ! in what darksome paths,
What risk and toil, is led your little life !
Oh, deaf to Nature's voice, that asks no more
Than body free from pain, that mind untouched

By cares and fear, in sweet repose enjoyed !
But few the wants of this our fleshly frame,
Few the possessions needful to confer
Freedom from pain, with many varied joys.
E'en these, at times, benignant Nature's hand
Unasked supplies.   What though throughout our
    halls
No youthful forms, in golden mould, illume
With lamps in outstretched hand, the midnight feast ;
Nor to the lyre resounds the gilded dome ?
Yet stretch'd recumbent on the soft green turf,
By cooling rill refreshed, 'neath shady boughs,
We taste unbought the daintiest joys of life ;
Most chiefly then when smiling Summer clothes
With varied flowers all the verdant meads.
Hot fevers quit not sooner painted quilts
And crimson canopies than common sheets.

    Since, then, nor pride of birth, nor rich attire,
Can ease our body's pain, nor regal state :
Still less can such things profit aught the soul.
Unless, forsooth, thou tell'st me that the sight
Of legions, all thine own, in martial form
Rang'd o'er the plain, of winged fleets that sweep

O'er Ocean's vast expanse, can from thy Soul
Chase Death's fell image, and the natural qualms
Of craven Superstition, while within
Reigns careless peace of mind, and sweet repose:
Why then 'twere well: but should experience sage
Blow notions such as these to empty winds,
Teaching, stern mistress! that relentless cares,
And swift-pursuing fears nor dread the ring
Of brazen armour, nor the clash of swords,
Respectless of crown'd heads and dignitaries,
Undazzled by the sheen of purple robes;
What hold we these but painted vanities,
Which idly strut when Reason hides her head?
In one long mental night we live; like boys
In darkness ever dreading fancied ills,
E'en so, in daylight broad, grown children, we
Affright our souls with images as real
As boyish bugbears conjured up by night.
This sombre veil to pierce, no solar rays
Are needed, nor the lucid shafts of day;
But Nature's light by Reason's mirror shown.

Now to my task.   In what perpetual round
The generating germs of things create

New forms, and old dissolve ; by what strange force
Impelled, and how for ever guided sure,
By laws unerring, through the realms of Space ;
These things now pour I to thy listening ear.
Most certain this, that no material form
Is held compact by bonds indissoluble.
All things of Earth we see grow less, by age
Dissolving slow, till Time's oblivious stream
Bears out of sight their gently lessening shapes :
Nathless, the Sum of Things remains the same,
Untouched by change ; for ever-lessening bulk
Quits its old shape but to augment a new,
Compelling this to flourish, that to wane,
In one place settled never : thus the whole
Is evermore renew'd, while nought is lost.
Thus breathing things live on by mutual waste
And gain kept up ; this dies that that may live,
This race declines, that grows; quick shifts the scene :
Like runners in the Games, we yield our place
To next in turn, the vital torch transferred.
Should'st think that these atomic germs can rest,
And, resting, thus give rise to motions new,
Thou widely err'st ; for, since through Space they
    range,

Most sure each atom must be borne along
By its own weight, or impetus of others :
What atoms with opposing motions meet
In diverse paths fly off, and further those
Most solid, for they no resistance meet
Of equal force.   But clearly to conceive
This endless whirl of all material shapes,
Forget not, friend, that in the Universe
No lowest point exists, no resting place
For these all-wandering primeval germs.
Space knows not form nor bound, stretch'd forth forth
    immense
T'wards every part alike ; as shown before
In long discussion, stor'd with ample proofs.
It follows that these atoms rest not, borne
For ever through th' unfathomable void
With varied ceaseless motion, such as meet
In altered course rebounding from the stroke.
Those which small space rebound, by distances
Minute removed, entangled into one
By closely-fitted shapes, form stony germs
And roots of iron ore—things most compact :
While others, in their wanderings less confined,
Form subtle air, and the Sun's dazzling light.

And other things there are that range though Space
Dismissed from Nature's workshop all unfit
With any form created to unite.
Of this, before our eyes an instance apt
Spontaneous offers on each sunny day.
For mark, from crevice small when daylight pours
Into a darksome vault, what endless maze
Thou see'st of atoms in th' injected beams,
Wheeling in mimic fight with endless whirl,
These singly, those in troops; in discord all
Perpetual borne, without a moment's pause.
From these thou may'st conjecture what the germs
Of all things are, and how through Space they whirl.
Thus small things may give instances of great,
Thus traces faint may lead to Science' path.
To thoughts far deeper should thy mind be led
By this atomic dance in noon-tide rays,
These motions of things palpable to sight
Suggesting others underneath, unseen.
Mark'st not, how, struck aside by unseen blow,
Anon these little bodies change their route,
Anon fly back, in all directions urg'd ?
Of this eternal maze the latent spring
Lies in the first-born germs with motion fraught

Spontaneous; next to these, small bodies form'd
Of fewest particles, whose essences
Nearest approach the first, are hurried on
By stroke unseen of particles first born:
These, in their turn, impel the next in rank:
Thus motion, from its base ascending slow,
By measured steps mounts upwards to our sight,
Till to those forms it reaches which we see
In sunbeams dancing, by what force unknown.

Next, friend, from observations few we trace
How swiftly move these same primordial germs.
When first Aurora sheds her new-born light
O'er all the land, awakening into song
The fluttering warblers of the trackless woods,
Who needs be told, when o'er the mountain top
Sol rears his crest, with what impetuous speed
His winged beams shoot forth to fill the World?
But not through empty Space they pass, compelled
To cleave their way through thin aërial waves,
Shorn of their speed in part; again, complex
Into each other twin'd, not simple forms,
They mutual hindrance make; thus from without,
At once, and from within, their race is check'd:

Whereas first atoms, simple in their shape,
And solid, borne through realms of empty void
Unchecked unhindered to their destin'd goal,
Must in their race outstrip Sol's tardy rays,
Through vaster regions hurried in what time
These slowly traverse this our little Sky;
For ne'er by thinking soul can these first germs
Be stopp'd, nor have they power themselves to stay
Enquiring into laws by which they move.

There are who witless hold that Nature's course
Could not, without the agency of Gods,
Be modelled thus subservient to our wants,
Nor Seasons run their round, nor fruits spring forth;
That not to chance we owe that joy Divine
That peoples the wide World, to countless Time
Prolonging man's frail race; hence straight they feign
Gods authors of the World, and all therein:
Far wandering from the truth, with pain mis-spent.
For though I knew not what the germs of things
Are in their Nature, yet, from proofs drawn down
From Heaven itself, thick multiplied o'er Earth,
I dare affirm this same material World
Made by no Gods, and never made for us,

ON THE NATURE OF THINGS. 61

By evil all corrupt: of this anon.
Atomic motions now demand our thought.

This seems the most convenient place to show
That nothing, of its own peculiar force,
Can upwards move, and wander through the Skies.
Let not the forms of flame deceive thy sight,
Which upwards spring new-born, and upwards grow,
Nor upward-shooting trees, that to the Sky
Rear their fair fruit : for know that every weight
(And all things weight possess) must downwards tend :
Nor deem erroneous when thou see'st the flames
Leap to thy topmost roof, with forked tongue
Devouring all they meet, that of their will
They act not urged by any force below :
A kindred force they own to that which spouts
The purple stream on high from open'd vein.
See'st not how force of fluids presses up
Light corks and wood ? The more thine eager hand
Would press them down unwilling, yet the more
The elastic fluid, angry, shoots them up,
Forcing to light e'en more than half their bulk.
Yet doubt we not that through an empty Space
These bodies, of themselves, would downwards move.

This instance mark'd, we judge how flames may rise,
By force beneath up-urged ; though by their weight,
(Such weight as flames possess) they downwards tend.
But mark how through the Heavens devious fly
Wide flakes of liquid flame, to right and left
Wheeling in rapid course : mark how to Earth
Fall shooting fiery globes : and how the Sun
Pours from the highest pinnacle of Heaven
His rays all-searching through the gilded fields,
With downward motion prone : and how the Clouds,
Surcharg'd with fiery wrath, encountering, pour
Their crackling vollies all across the Skies :
From all these signs, what judge we but that Fire
Seeks not to rise, but rather downwards tends ?

Next know, my friend, that every primal germ
Which falls through vacuum downwards, veers its
        course
A little devious from the strict right line ;
The times and the degrees of change unknown,
Enough that thou may'st say it falls not straight.
For simple reason that, like dropping shower,
Without such small deflexion, every germ
Would to the boundless deep rush headlong down

In parallel descent, no issue join'd :
Thus nought that is would ever have been formed.

Should any think that germs of heavier weight
Can fall on lighter from above, borne down
With greater speed, creating other shocks,
With novel generating motions fraught ;
He wanders far from Reason's simple path.
What things indeed through Air or Water fall,
With swiftness fall proportion'd to their weight,
For reason plain, that fluid's substance rare,
Resists not all things equally, cut through
With greatest ease by bodies most compact.
Whereas pure Void, indifferent alike
To weight or lightness, no resistance makes
To aught that through it, urg'd by Nature, falls.
Thus all things, of necessity, through void,
Of weights diverse, with equal speed descend.
Nor can the heavier atom from above
Fall on the light beneath, creating strokes
With novel generating motions fraught.
It follows that all bodies fall inclin'd,
But in degree minutest, lest we feign
Motions oblique, and that the fact refutes.

For ample observation shows that weights
Descending cannot wander from their course,
Borne down before our eyes in line direct,
But this minute deflexion who shall trace?
What mortal eye shall dare mark out the line?

But lastly, ask we how, if motion all
Is in one chain unbroken, each new link
Form'd as the last, in order infinite,
If never the primordial germs of things,
Verging together, combinations form,
First interruptions of Fate's stern decrees,
Forbidding cause to follow cause, in round
Eternal: how to living things belongs
This will, all free to act, unforced by Fate,
Which leads us all where Pleasure shows the way?
Our motions bend we not, unchain'd by Time,
By place uncircumscrib'd, where Fancy leads?
'Tis certain each his own free will directs:
Hence Motion springs, through all the limbs diffused.
Mark how, the barrier loos'd, th' impetuous steed,
All panting for the strife, would instant rush,
But, for a moment cannot—wherefore this?
'Tis that short moment into action stirs

Th' atomic troops within the frame, arrang'd
In order, to attend the will's commands.
You see that from the heart all Motion springs,
Set going by the mind's free will; diffus'd
Thence through the frame, and every quivering limb.
Other the motions caused by forceful stroke
Our strength o'erpowering : then the unruly limbs
Move against orders urged by foreign force
Until the will deposed resumes its sway.
Thou markest how, though man may oft be borne
And hurried on precipitate by power
External 'gainst his will, yet deep within
His breast lies that which fights, if not prevails ?
Which in its turn redeems the impressed troops
From captive thrall, back to its post assign'd,
Each distant calls, and rules through every limb ?
Hence to seeds also we must needs assign
Besides both weight and casual strokes, a cause
Whence springs this power: for nought of nothing
     comes.
For weight forbids that by these casual strokes
As 'twere by force external things be made :
But that a dire necessity within
The mind herself should over-rule her acts,

This slight declension of atomic parts
Prevents, uncertain both in place and time.

Nor was the total mass e'er more compact,
Or e'er remov'd by greater intervals :
For, added nothing, nothing e'er falls off.
Wherefore what motion all these seeds of things
Primordial have, that had they in all time,
That will they have for ever : and what things
Rise into being now, such e'er will rise
In self-same mould renew'd, and wax in strength
To the degree assigned by Nature's law.
There is no force to change the sum of things.
There is no place within the Universe
To which stray matter can escape, or whence
Can burst a power unknown, to interrupt
The course of things, and new creations form.

Nor wonder, friend, that while the primal germs
For ever move, the whole should seem at rest,
Motions of each peculiar thing except.
Full many a fathom 'neath our senses ken,
Lies deep the nature of primordial things.
Then how would'st trace the motions infinite

Of things themselves not palpable to sight?
E'en things thou seest oft move unknown to thee,
By Space to distances obscure removed.
Mark well yon fleecy flock, that o'er the hill
For pasture ranges wild, as each invites
Herbage most green with freshest dew-drops gemmed,
While frisk the well-fed lambkins o'er the turf.
Now shift the scene to far; thou seest a speck
Of white on the green hill side, nothing more.
Again, when mighty legions fill the plain,
Marching in pomp of war; their burnish'd arms
Flashing to Heaven, while the earth around
Glitters all brazen, and the tramp of feet
And mighty roar of men is borne aloft
To mountain tops, thence echoed to the stars,
And wheeling hither thither o'er the plain
Swift horsemen shake the ground with thundering
        hoof.
And yet there is a spot on yon blue height,
Whence all this turmoil seems at rest, beheld
A glittering speck on the extended plain.

  Explore we now what are the first-born germs
Of all things made, and how diverse in form,

5 *

Scatter'd through Space in varied shapes profuse :
'Tis not that many differ, but the rule
Is difference, not sameness ; nor does this
Aught wond'rous seem, their numbers such that end
And sum they know not, as already shown.
Strange, rather, should such countless myriads all
Of texture like consist, and form the same.

Of man's proud race, of all the scaly tribes
Mute tenants of the deep, of bleating flocks,
Of ravenous prowlers of the woods, of birds
That sing in pleasant places by still lakes
Or rivers, or sweet gushing springs, and those
That haunt the lone recesses of deep woods,
Of all these infinite take one, and where
It follow shalt thou find in all things match'd ?
This difference 'tis whereby the mother knows
Her babe, the babe its mother : nor with sense
Less nice than human knows the dam her young.

Lo by the altar's side, in column'd court
Of yon proud Fane, where curls the perfumed smoke,
The dying calf spurts forth the purple tide.
Him seeks his dam bereaved o'er the green lawns

Tracing the cleft marks of the well known hoofs,
And searching all around with wistful eyes
For her lost loved one, while the leafy grove
She fills with plaintive moans, returning oft
In lingering hope to the accustomed stalls.
Her nor green herbs delight with dew-drops deck'd,
Nor willows waving o'er the brimming stream,
One image only fills her absent thoughts,
Nor through the pasture gay can one be found
Her cares to soothe, her lost hope to replace:
So yearns her heart for one, and that her own.
E'en so, with plaintive voice, the little kids
Seek each its horned dam, the sportive lambs
Their well-known ewes; thus, urg'd by natural
      laws,
Each draws its food from the congenial spring.
And last, nor ears of corn, when view'd minute,
Thou find'st resembling each in every part:
Nor shells that paint Earth's bosom when the Sea
Waters with rippling waves the thirsty sand.
And so throughout wide Nature: hence, most sure,
Th' essential germs, to no one pattern made
By artificial hand, all freely range,
In varied forms, throughout the realms of Space.

Hence may we solve the question why *that* Fire
Offspring of Thunder, should far deeper pierce
Than our dull flames, of earthly torches born.
Of subtler essence is that Heaven-born fire,
Of finer particles composed that pierce
Through openings which our grosser flames impede.
Again, through horny substance daylight shines,
From which rebounds the shower : and why ? but that
More gross the parts of Water than of Light.
Quick through the strainer glides the trickling wine,
That oil more slow retards : for oil consists
Of grosser elemental particles,
More closely hook'd together, more entwined ;
So from its neighbour each primordial seed
More slowly disunited, finds its way
With painful course through its peculiar pore.
Hence comes it that with pleasing taste the tongue
Imbibes soft milk and honey : while sharp rue
And wormwood writhe the countenance with pain.
Hence to thy mind 'tis clear, of atoms round
And smooth created things that please our sense :
While of more crooked particles composed
Those we call sharp and bitter, with rude force
Tearing the film o'er our senses spread.

All things, to sum our argument, that please
Or wound the sense, of differing germs are made :
Nor deem the horrors of the grating saw
Of things composed as smooth as those sweet sounds
Awak'd by cunning fingers on the lyre :
Nor that the rotting carcase to our smell
Sends particles of form the same as those
That from Silician saffron scattered rise,
Or altars with Panchæan incense spread.
Nor deem of seeds the same rich colours made,
That feast th' enraptur'd eye, and those foul
        forms,
And combinations hideous, that wound
The injured sight, and force th' unwilling tears.
This know, that nothing can delight the sense
But by some smoothness of its primal germs :
Nor less that each thing harshest and most rude,
To atoms rough its form repulsive owes.

Yet things there are that can be held nor smooth
Nor altogether hook'd, with points close twin'd,
But shaped in angles rather, on all sides
Outjutting, that more teaze than hurt the sense :
Such acid pickles made from dregs of wine.

And last, our touch proclaims that fiery heat
And pinching wint'ry frost, extremes diverse,
Both bite severe, though armed with different fangs.

Touch is the sense of senses—O, ye Gods!—
In every part diffused, alike acute
To that which enters from without, and that
Which, inborn, issuing forth, gives pain or joy:
Nor less to atoms in the frame, uprous'd
To strife intestine by external stroke:
Dost doubt?   Then strike with bended fist where'er
Thy fancy wills, th' effect thou straight shalt prove.
Hence, then, the same conclusion; that what things
Cause different sense, of differing germs consist.

To sum our case, those things most hard and dense
Of germs must needs be form'd most intertwin'd,
Held, as it were, compact by woven boughs.
First in the ranks comes adamant, unhurt
By puny blows contemn'd, and hardy flints:
Stern iron's ruthless strength, and solid brass,
Whose grating staples hold the ponderous bolts.
But things of fluid or of liquid bulk
Of particles more round and smooth consist;
Soft trickling down, impeded by no parts

In their primordial texture intertwin'd.
And last, what things thou see'st disperse in Air,
As smoke, and mist, and flames consist of parts,
If not all smooth and round, yet not held fast
By close entanglement : but free to pierce
The human frame and looser substances,
Without cohesion in themselves, because
Of pointed atoms made not intertwined.

Nor wond'rous let it seem, if some few things
Be pungent both, and fluid, as the brine
Of the salt Ocean : for though fluids all
Of parts both round and smooth consist, combin'd,
When pungent as the Sea, with painful parts,
Yet not of strict necessity entwin'd
With hooked points these painful germs, globose
Perchance, and flowing with the others free
In motion fraught with evil to the sense.
To prove that bitterness of Neptune's tide
Is caused by mixture of the smooth and rough,
Behold a test appealing to thy sense.
View where the briny Sea, distill'd through Earth
Or porous sand, drops sweet into the bed
Of yonder pool ; its particles saline
Entrapp'd in meshes of the filtering bank.

This prov'd, next come we to an inference
That rises straight from demonstrations past.
'Tis this : that all variety of shapes
Of primal things is finite; for, if not,
Would some first things be infinite in bulk.
The size minute of first atomic germs
Admit not great variety of change :
Assume three forms, or even more, yet more,
These twist to right and left, turn up or down,
Transpose in every mode their shape admits;
At last it comes to this—if farther change
Thou would'st, 'tis needful to combine more
    parts;
Of these the combinations all used up,
Yet more thou fain must ask, if yet thou would'st
More shapes : thus follows novelty of form
Increase of bulk; nor can'st thou infinite
Maintain the shapes of seeds lest forc'd to own
Existing some of magnitude immense,
Which I have shown impossible before.

Why then barbarian tunics, and the gloss
Of Melibœan purple rich distill'd
From shells Thessalian, and the gorgeous hues
That flash and sparkle from the peacock's tail

Would all unheeded lie, surpassed by tint
More gorgeous still : despised would be the scent
Of myrrh, sweet honey's taste, the dulcet notes
Of dying swan, e'en the most cunning strains
By Phœbus' self awaken'd on the lyre,
Would for like cause seem dead and vapid all :
For something new would still superior rise.
Nor less from bad to worse would all things tend ;
No worst in Nature more than best : thus each
Offensive thing, to taste, or sight, or smell,
Could not be most offensive ; still some worse.
But 'tis not so ; for both extremes finite
Exist of things that wound the sense or please ;
Hence, also, finite the primordial shapes.

And lastly, trace the track from heat to cold ;
Thou com'st to ice, and can'st no further go,
So back again to fire ; 'twixt ice and fire
Degrees lie various to fill up the scale.
Not infinite the range of heat and cold,
But by strict limits guarded : fire and frost
Stand sentinel at either extreme bound.
This prov'd, next come we to an inference
That, following closely join'd, must win our faith :

'Tis this: that all first germs, of shape the same,
Are infinite; for since the shapes themselves
Are finite, were the germs of every shape
In number finite also, then the whole
Were finite; which I have before disprov'd,
When I set forth the motions infinite,
With ever renovating power fraught
Of primal germs, from th' eternal past
In endless chain brought down, which numberless,
Have fill'd, and fill th' Immensity of Space.

Though certain animals more rare appear,
And Nature seems less fruitful of their kind,
It may be that in other distant lands
And climes more genial she fills up the tale.
Thus elephants, snake-handed, first of beasts,
With ivory rampart fence the realms of Ind,
On every side impervious, such their host,
Though known to us by specimens but rare.
But should I this concede, that one sole form
May in the Universe unique consist,
To other living thing unlike: how then?
If not unbounded the material germs
Conceiving and producing, never then

This monstrous form had been created, never,
Created, could it have increased and lived.
Should I this too concede that primal germs
Finite of some one thing may float through Space :
Where, when, how forc'd, by what design, should such
Materials, floating on the boundless sea
Of heterogeneous things combine in one ?
I know no means by which they can combine :
But as the angry Ocean scatters wide,
In wrath aroused, masts, benches, rudders, oars,
And prows and gilded poops, on devious waves
Promiscuous borne to many a distant shore,
To warn rash mortals of the tempting deep
That woos them to their fate, by signs foreshown
Of treachery and violence hid beneath
The smiles insidious of the wanton sea :
So finite should'st thou hold of any things
The germs primordial, them through endless Space
Would scatter, hither, thither, the wide waves
Of the material ocean infinite;
Forbidding that they join combin'd by plan,
Or, once conjoin'd, remain, or grow in bulk.
Thus nought would have been made, or, made, have
    grown.

'Tis proved that infinite of every kind
Are primal germs from whence all things proceed.

Nor can destructive motions for all time
Prevail, all life entombing evermore,
Nor motions making and preserving keep
Created things for ever : rages thus
Of principles antagonist the war
From infinite begun, with dubious strife.
Now here, now there, the vital powers prevail,
Sometimes o'ermastered : with funereal dirge
Are blended puny cries of new-born babes :
Nor follows day one night, nor night one dawn,
That hears not, mingled with infantine wails
The shrieks of woe attendants of the tomb.

Moreover, on these thoughts intent, know this,
And known, deep grave within thy mind, that
　　naught
By Nature to our senses shown, is made
Of but one sort of primal particles,
But all of mingled seeds; of forces those
And attributes most varied, of most parts,
In nature differing, as in form unlike.

And first, within her womb those essences
Contains the teeming Earth whence rise cool springs,
That, rolling on in rivers e'er renew
Th' immeasurable Ocean ; whence quick fires,
These scorching the parch'd ground beneath, while
  those
Impetuous blaze from Ætna's fiery throat.
And yet another fount she holds, whence spring
Rich crops and joyous trees that nourish man,
And glad his senses ; nor with bounty less
Sheds she glad pastures, leaves, and brooks to feed
The untam'd mountain herds ; hence mother nam'd
Of Gods and men alike, and bestial tribes.
Her sung the learned bards of classic Greece
Two lions curbing on her car sublime,
Teaching that this our world hangs pois'd in Air,
Nor (notion vain) that Earth on Earth can rest.
The yoked lions told that cubs most fierce
May yet be softened by parental care.
A mural crown adorn'd her lofty brow,
For that proud cities she protects with towers ;
Thus crown'd, e'en now in awful state revered,
Is borne our mother's idol through the world.
Her nations various, after ancient forms,

Idæan mother call, while Phrygian troops
With dance and song surround her stately car :
Because (so says the tale) in Phrygia first
Sprang fruits, thence wide diffused throughout the
    world.
And Eunuch Priests they give her ; symbols these
That all untouch'd by filial piety
To their first parent, or to those ingrate
From whom their fount of life immediate sprang,
Themselves unworthy to produce to light
Aught living progeny : with frequent hands
They beat the hollow cymbals, the loud drums
Resound, and brays the hoarse harsh threatening horn,
While stir up to the dance shrill Phrygian pipes :
And spears they brandish emblems of fierce rage
To fright the rabble's unbelieving heart,
And soul ingrate, with dire religious awe.
Her hail mankind, as, through proud cities borne,
She rides triumphant, scattering gifts around,
Though mute, benign : with brass profuse they pave,
And silver strewn, the ways ; thick o'er the crowd
Of nymphs attendant rains the roseate shower ;
Around her troop a band, surnamed by Greeks
Curetes Phrygian, for they dance full arm'd

Dripping with blood, and wave their frightful crests
With gestures furious to the maddening strains,
Like those Curetes old, Dictæans named,
Who erst in Crete with martial music drown'd
The cries of infant Jove.   With nimble foot
Around him danc'd a choir of youths full arm'd,
Their shields quick clashing to the measur'd tune,
Lest ruthless Saturn should devour the babe,
And pierce with cureless wound the mother's heart.
Hence follows arm'd the troop, or arm'd, perchance,
To typify the Goddess' high behest,
That all with valour and with arms the State
Defend, and guard their parent's hoary head.

'Tis well: such glittering shows may please the
     sense,
But Reason shocked from that vain crowd retires.
Most sure the Nature of the Gods enjoys
Within itself Immortal Life, in peace
Profound, from human cares far, far remote;
Sublimely passionless, and in itself
For all things all-sufficient, pain and fear
It knows not, nor requires it ought of us,
Nor pleased by virtue, nor provoked by crime.

6

There are who call the Sea by Neptune's name,
And crops by name of Ceres: who prefer
To miscall " Bacchus " what is rightly wine.
Grant we to such if so their fancy wills
That they call Earth the Mother of the Gods,
So that in sober earnest they forbear
With foul religion to pollute the mind.

But to resume our argument : mark well,
In the same pasture both the fleecy flocks
And the young war-horse reared, and lowing herds,
All 'neath the same wide canopy of Heaven,
Their thirst all slaking from the self-same stream ;
Yet each its form generic holding, each
Its sire's propensities ; such various germs,
With various natures sympathetic, live
In every kind of grass, in every stream.
Yet more: combined in every living form
Dwell bones and muscles, blood, veins, bowels, heat
And moisture : properties far differing, all
Of divers elemental parts composed.
Again, the blazing pile shows hidden seeds
Of flame, if of nought else, within itself

Conceal'd till call'd to light, then bursting forth
In crackling sparks, and ashes widely strewn.

All nature analyzing thus thou find'st
That every body holds of many things
The latent seeds, these seeds of various forms.

And, lastly, things thou see'st endued with
    scent,
And taste, and colour, all at once, these parts
Each made of its own germs : thus penetrates
The scent where colour enters not, while taste
Affects our senses in a different way :
Hence of each different the primal germs.
Thus forms unlike into one compact whole
Combine, and things of mingled seeds consist.

Again, in this our verse, to many a word
Full many a common element thou see'st ;
Yet words and verses own'st thou different, each
Of different Elements made up : 'tis not
That many a letter is not common, or
No different words of self-same letters made ;
But that, as wholes, the words are different :

6 *

And so in other things, though common all
Or most composing germs, unlike the sum.
For simple, into complex form'd, acquire
New essences : thus may'st thou call man's race,
And fruit, and shrubs, of different germs composed.
Yet dream not that all germs may join with all
Promiscuous : to thy sight what portents dire
Would rise! half bestial forms, half stately man!
From human trunks upreared high-towering boughs,
Terrestrial limbs joined on to fins and scales,
And hideous-jawed Chimæras breathing flames
By Nature reared on all-producing Earth.
Yet nothing monstrous view we ; by fixed laws
Of atoms fixed since things are made, and made
With power endued their race begun to keep.
Those laws of stern necessity unchanged :
For of all food that enters in, the germs
In various ways diverge, each seeking those
Congenial, which, straight found, combining, raise
Th' appropriate motions : other alien germs
Repulsive Nature casts to earth, or forced
Through every pore minute emits unseen,
Unapt to join with any, all uncouth
To whirl harmonious in the vital dance.

Nor deem these laws to sentient things alone
Confin'd—throughout all Nature wide diffus'd :
For, of necessity, each differing form
Is made of primal germs of different shapes.
'Tis not that many are not similar ;
But false that all resemble all : again,
As the seeds differ, different intervals
Must separate the parts, and different strokes
Connecting or disjoining rise, and weights
And motions ; thus not animals alone
Distinct in form creating, but the Sea
From Earth dividing, from the Sea the Sky.

Now listen to my song, with labour sweet
That gathers honied truths from things observ'd.
Nor deem, untaught, of white primordial seeds
White things created : nor of black, things black :
Nor that aught seen, of any colour, owes
Its hue to that of its essential germs.
The primal parts of Matter colourless
Exist, nor like, nor unlike, objects seen.
But hold'st thou to the mind impalpable
These hueless germs ?   Thou widely err'st from
        Truth.

Conceives not in his mind the man born blind
The ideas of bodies touch'd, from infancy
With colour unassociated ? hence
Conceive how may be imaged to our mind
The forms of hueless things : e'en in the dark,
Things without colour by the touch we know.
Such may be, then ; now prove we that it must.
Though every colour changes, yet the germs
Primæval change not ever ; for, were naught
Immutable, all things would come to naught :
When anything diverges from its bounds,
Follows the death of that it was before :
Have care, then, how thou paint'st the germs of
    things,
Lest thy fell brush annihilate the World.
But if all colourless the germs of things,
By varied forms producing various hues,
As each with each, by chance position join'd,
Receives or gives impressions ; simple then
The cause whence that which was this moment black
Marmoreal whiteness takes, abruptly chang'd :
As when the Sea, by angry winds uprous'd,
Changes its green wave to white fleecy foam ;
For then would'st say that what we see most dark,

Its primal particles uprous'd, their ranks
Confused, perchance some lost, or added some,
By metamorphose sudden white becomes.
Of germs cerulean were the Sea made up
Its waves could never whiten; stir them up
Howe'er thou would'st, the blue must blue remain.
But were those primal germs of various hues,
Which mix'd make up the whiteness of the foam,
As different forms and parts with judgment mix'd
May make a simple square, and as, in squares
So form'd, the parts component we may see,
So in the Sea's pure white we should perceive
The different hues that, mixed, make up the whole.
Moreover, nothing hinders but that forms
Diverse should join one simple to create;
But diverse colours cannot by like rules
Be join'd, nor forced, in parts, to make an whole.

E'en could they be, yet still the proof remains
That seeds are colourless: since of white germs
Things white are not composed, nor black of black,
But each of varied seeds: and white things spring
More readily from nothing than from black,
Or any other contradicting hue.

Again, since without light hues cannot live,
Nor palpable to light are primal germs,
'Tis obvious primal germs no colour know.
In total darkness, what can colour be?
Existence fickle, that in very light
For ever varies, as by rays oblique
Or straight impressed. The soft and changeful
    down
That clothes the dove's sleek throat and burnished
    crest
Now flashes in the Sun with ruddy glow
Of bright pyropus, while anon it seems
To mingle emerald's green with coral red.
E'en so the peacock's tail in midday light
Changes its colours as it meets the Sun.
Such colours, then, by certain unknown force
Of light produced, without light ne'er had been.
Again, some certain stroke our eye receives
When, in our phrase, it sees an object white ;
When black another, so the same throughout.
And by the touch we objects recognize
As figured, not as tinted : thus 'tis clear
No hues are needed to primordial germs,
By varied shapes producing varied strokes.

Yet more, since not by certain shapes confin'd
Is colour in its nature, and since all
Primordial forms may be of every hue,
Why not things form'd of germs, as germs themselves,
Of every colour intermixed made up?
Thus, on white wings might fly the sombre crow,
And swans in mourning swim, with any hue
Or hues endow'd, by blindest chance combin'd.
Again, by how much into parts minute
Is subdivided anything, so much
Its colour loses it by slow degrees :
Behold a piece of purple torn to shreds—
The filaments, combined of richest hue,
Dispersed, their colour lose : from this 'tis shown
That particles of all things lose their hues
Before they vanish to primordial seeds.

And, lastly, since thou own'st that sound and smell
All bodies sent not forth, and thus to some
These properties deniest : since, again,
That we see all things is not prov'd : confess
That some things without colour are, as some
Inodorous and mute, nor these than those
Grasped with less ease by the sagacious mind.

But not of colour only are bereft
Primæval bodies, but of warmth and cold,
And heated moisture ; sterile of all sound,
By juice unmoisten'd, with no odour fraught.
Thus who would balmy liquid make of myrrh
Or flower of spikenard, or sweet marjoram,
Nectarean odour breathing, he must mix
The spicy elements with olive oil
Inodorous, lest the vehicle that holds
Dissolv'd these scents should mar the rich compound.
So seeds, main substance of created things,
Cannot impart to bodies, of themselves,
Or smell, or sound, or savour, or moist heat :
For changeable are all these properties,
And all the bodies that possess them die,
Or soft, or hard, or dense, obnoxious all
To putrefaction and mortality.
These, then, from seeds thou fain must separate,
If to the Sum of Things a principle
Thou giv'st immortal and unchangeable :
If not, to nothing all would straight return.

Now, further, strict necessity compels
That we hold all things sentient produced

Of germs insensible : nor well known facts
This theory refute, or e'en oppose,
But rather, rightly view'd, to the belief
Lead on by gentle steps that, as I say,
Of things insensate sentient things are form'd.
Thou see'st in filth bred living worms, when Earth,
With wet unseasonable decomposed,
Grows putrid : all things in a round thou see'st
Of change perpetual, pleasant pastures, leaves
And rivers into cattle changed, and changed
Cattle to man : while we again in turn
Contribute to invigorate the frames
Of beasts, or pass into the plumes of birds.
Thus into living bodies every food
Enchantress Nature changes, and compounds
Of animals the senses : with like skill,
Though greater, as when into flames she blows
Like crackling wood, and changes all to fire.
Now see'st thou how important 'tis to know
The order in which primal germs are placed
And how commixed they motions give and take ?
Why, then ? How, then ? What is it that thy mind
Perplexes ? Whence that deep repugnance felt
To own things sentient of insensate born ?

Most true, nor stone, nor wood, nor earth, mix'd up,
Can vital sense impart : remember that
I say not sense can be produced straight forth
From every combination of first germs :
But that the secret spell that calls up sense
Lies in the numbers and the combinations,
Figures and motions, of the primal parts.
All these in wood exist not, nor in clay,
And yet e'en these, when putrified by wet,
With maggots teem : because, the order chang'd
And decomposed of their primæval parts,
These newly mixed the living power acquire.

But those that hold things sensible made up
Of sentient germs, these germs, then, soft must hold :
For every sense is closely join'd with nerves,
And veins, and bowels, all in body soft
United, and obnoxious all to death.
But feign them all eternal : be it so :
Then they possess each of some part the sense,
Or each, as the whole sentient thing, must feel.
But, of themselves, the parts can never feel,
For each demands the fellowship of all :
The hand lopp'd off is dead to every sense,

And so, without the body, every part.
It only then remains that every germ
Be liken'd to a total animal,
That feels throughout the vital sense : but how
Can every germ be called a primal part,
By death untouch'd, if germs are animals,
And animals and mortals are the same ?
But, were it so, then naught could they create
But motley crowds of living things : no more
Than men, wild beasts and cattle could create
Aught new by any kind of intercourse.
But if, transform'd, they lose their proper sense,
And take another, wherefore give them that
Which straight thou tak'st away ?   All facts compel
That to our first conclusion we return :
Both eggs of birds to chickens chang'd, and worms
Upspringing from the wet and sodden Earth,
Proclaim things sentient of insensate born.

Should any hold that sentient from inert
Can only spring from some anterior change
Of parts, a separate birth in each before
Their combination : to refute them this
Suffices, clearly shown, that never birth

Can spring but from the juncture of first parts :
Nor without combinations different
Can any change arise : of nought that lives
Exists the sense before combined the parts
That make the nature of the animal,
Scattered in sooth before through Air, and Earth,
And Water, in confusion infinite,
As yet unmix'd together, unendued
With vital motion, whence our senses flow.

Again, a heavier stroke than Nature bears
Makes sudden havoc, and the sentient parts
Of mind and body in confusion throws ;
The organized position of the parts
All broken up, and stopp'd the vital pulse :
Then all the stuff of which our life is made,
Shaken and jumbled through each limb, unties
The vital knot wherein the soul consists,
And forces out our life through every pore.
Now what more power can a blow possess
Than to dissolve or shake things placed in form ?
Not seldom see we, after stroke less strong,
Life's scatter'd forces rally and prevail ;
Th' uproused sedition quelling, and each part

Rebellious back recalling to its ranks:
Life in the body then, o'er Death's short sway
Prevailing, kindles each extinguish'd sense.
What power but this could the departing germs
Of Life force backward from the gates of Death,
His portals closing till the appointed time ?
Again, since pain arises when the germs
Throughout the body are disturb'd and shook,
In limb, or vein, or nerve ; but back restored
To order, pleasure straight succeeds to grief :
From this we know these same primordial germs
Insensible to pleasure in themselves,
Nor less to pain : for they are of no parts
Which mov'd, disturb'd, or disarrang'd, can e'er
Affect them sensibly, nor pleasure give
By any combination pleasurable :
Hence without sense are all primordial germs.

Last, if each sense which to each living thing
Belongs is to be given to their germs—
What ?—of what germs, then, is man's nature made ?
That now with laughter shakes, now changeful pours
Grief's tearful stream adown the moisten'd cheeks :
That has the power withal to search the springs

Of Nature, and its own component seeds.

Since, then, these germs are like whole animals,
They must themselves of different parts consist ;
These parts of others, nor can'st ever stop :
Thus when thou speak'st, or laugh'st, or think'st
    profound,
By speaking, laughing, thinking germs thou act'st.
But should all this appear absurd and vain,
Should a man laugh not made of laughing germs,
And think profound, and clothe his thoughts in words,
By no germs aided wise or eloquent :
Why, then, should bodies sentient not be made
Of primal germs, themselves insensate all ?

Again, we all from seed Celestial spring—
Our Father in the Heavens—whence fair Earth
Imbibing gentle moisture, pregnant grows,
And, in their season, brings forth goodly fruits,
And trees, and every beast, and sovereign man ;
With food congenial all her helpless young
Supplying bounteous, that each blithe may live
Its little life, and propagate its kind :
Whence has she justly earn'd the mother's name.
But that which came from Earth to Earth returns ;

While all from Heaven distill'd, to Heaven again
Upwafted, the Celestial temples hold.
'Tis not that Death can the component parts
Of things destroy, but their arrangement change ;
Things joining strange before, and causing that
All bodies change their forms, their colours blend,
And senses take, and in fit time return.
Hence may'st thou see how the same primal germs,
Newly combined and placed, and motions new
Receiving both and giving, may create
Unnumber'd forms, in moulds unnumber'd cast.

  Nor not eternal deem the atomic germs,
Because seen idly floating on the top
Of things material, born and straight dissolv'd.
In this our verse what vast effects arise
From words and letters variously combined !
The germs poetic, in most part the same
Their order changed unnumbered meanings give.
Analogy straight leads us to conceive
How, in things also, of the primal germs
The combinations, motions, distances,
Strokes, weights, concussions, and rebounds, and shapes
And order changed, results wide differing rise.

7

Now lend thy soul to Reason's truthful voice,
For shall thine ear a novel sound invade,
A novel sight thy mental eye shall pierce.
Nothing so simple that, when offered first
To the perception, is not hard of faith:
Nothing so great or wondrous but, in time
Familiar grown, our wonder dies away.
Take, for example, the pure azure vault
Studded with wandering Stars, the Moon's soft light,
And the more dazzling splendour of the Sun.
Conceive this glorious vision fresh revealed
Unknown, unlooked for, to the sight of man:
What could there be more wondrous? what, if told
By prophets, would the nations less believe?
Nothing, I ween; so marvellous 'twould appear!
And yet scarce one, of sights familiar tired,
Deigns to gaze upward to the glorious vault.
Cease, then, by simple novelty alarm'd,
To spurn with loathing reason from thy mind:
But weigh my words with jealous care: if true,
Give me thy hand: if false, be then my foe.

Since infinite the realms that lie beyond
The walls of this our world, we yearn to know

What dwells within those realms : the winged soul
Free soaring through all space would fain explore
The secrets of the vast and boundless deep.
For first, on every side, above, beneath,
There is no end, as I·have shown before,
Self-evident in truth, and from the essence
Inseparable of Infinity.
How, then, through such illimitable Space
Deem we innumerable atoms borne,
With every motion, through Eternal Time,
Potent to form but this our Earth and Sky ?
While all not used up here inertly roam
Through barren Space ? Why this our World is made,
By concourse all fortuitous, unplann'd,
Of bodies knock'd together, now in vain,
Now with concussion fortunate, till met
At last things apt in generating form,
Rise Earth, and Sea, and Sky, and sentient tribes.
Hence must we needs confess, in other parts,
Other conjunctions of material things,
Like this our World, throughout wide Ether spread.

In sooth, with all the implements prepared
The place at hand, and no impeding cause,

Things needs must of necessity be made.
Of germs such is the number that all life
Would not suffice to count them : and their force
And nature is unchangeable, all Space
With the same motions filling as our World.
Hence own that other Worlds exist in Space,
And other Men, and other Brutal Tribes.

Yet more, since of created things we see
Nothing unique, sole sample of its mould,
But each belonging to a class, and like
A thousand others ; this in mountain beasts
Observed alike, and men, and those mute tribes
That fill the deep, and birds that cleave the sky ;
Hence, by analogy compelled, confess
Earth, Sun, and Moon, and Sea, each thing that is,
One of a countless tribe : that laws the same
Call into being every greatest thing
And thing minutest ; nor, their race full run,
Waits this than that more sure the common grave.

By such philosophy assured, thou dar'st
View Nature acting freely, uncompell'd,
Unaided, e'en, by her proud Lords, the Gods.

For O, ye blessed souls of Powers above,
That lead your lives in all repose and peace,
Where is the Spirit, of Infinity
To rule the sum, with hand of force to guide
The reins of all the starry deep, each sky
Attempering to warm its fruitful Earth,
All present at all times ? with gathering clouds
Shrouding the firmament, or the blue serene
Shaking with thunder; while his towering fanes
He blasts with his own bolts ? now to the waste
Retreating sullen, his dread shafts to pour
With blinded fury on the insensate sand;
Those aimless shafts that oft at random strike
The good and just, while felons sleep secure ?

Since Earth's prime natal day, since first the Sun
Shot forth his beams, and Ocean bubbling rose,
To each have atoms ever flock'd, sent forth
On mission vague through Nature's teeming gulf,
Augmenting all ; whence gaining strength, the
    Heavens
Upreared aloft their towering battlements
High above Earth, and Air etherial rose.
For every atom borne from every part

In whirl perpetual, atoms finds at length
Congenial, and in its place subsides :
The wet with wet, Earthy with Earth conjoins,
And fiery fire, Etherial ether breeds.
Thus Nature, all-creating, to its size
Mature each body rears by slow degrees,
Till at that point arrived when not more flows
Into the vital veins than issues forth :
Such limit to each thing that lives assign'd,
Thus her own increase Nature moderate checks.
For all thou view'st in days of joyous youth
Waxing in conscious strength to force mature,
These more take in than dissipate, as yet
Their young veins kindly drinking in each food :
Nor blighting age has touch'd the fresh machine,
Scattering its parts diverse with greater speed
Than Nature renovates.   In constant flux
Lives everything : while more flows in than out,
Not yet has reach'd the frame its height mature :
Then Time his withering hand lays gently first
On strength adult which crumbles to decay.
Greater the bulk, th' increasing power remov'd,
More is the waste to every side diffus'd :
The food no longer kindly fills the veins,

Unequal to supply life's ebbing tide :
The needful food whereby all creatures live
Nature supplies not nor the veins receive.
By law thus perish all created things,
Life's tide out-flowing and their failing strength,
Harass'd and worn by never-ceasing jars
And blows and buffets of external force.
So shall the mighty walls that circle Earth,
By time o'erthrown, in dust and ruin lie.

E'en now our World is aged : Earth worn out,
With labour bears her puny sons, of old
Mother of giants, and huge monstrous beasts.
Those pretty tales let them believe who list,
That men were dropp'd by golden chain from Heaven,
Or born from clash of rocks with angry waves:
I hold that Earth, who rears them, first begat.

In palmy days of old, the Earth, yet young,
Spontaneous bore profuse the clustering vine,
And every fruit most fair ; throughout the fields
Rich pasture scattering wide, and golden grain,
That now ne'er springs unask'd, man's weary toil
Rewarding slow and sullen : the yok'd ox

We drive laborious, and the ploughman's strength
Waste on the clod that scarce our pain rewards.
Thus toil is more, its guerdon ever less.
Now shakes his head and sighs the aged swain,
Viewing his labours less and less avail,
While past with present he compares, and lauds
The lot more prosperous of his happier sire !
Planting the aged barren vine, on Time
He mutters curses, and th' unaiding Gods ;
Repeating oft how men of th' olden time,
Frugal and pious, bounded their small wants
By narrow strip of land, than acres now
More fertile ; while forgets his simple soul
That all things have their course, forespent by age
Slowly but surely sinking to the grave.

THE END.